Melodies for the Soul

Jessica Solchenberger

BookLeaf Publishing

India | USA | UK

Presentation by *BookLeaf Publishing*

Web: www.bookleafpub.com

E-mail: info@bookleafpub.com

ISBN: 9789363319622

First edition 2024

*To my Mom and Dad. Thank you for
always believing in me!*

ACKNOWLEDGEMENT

I'm thankful to my parents, brother and sister-in-law and nephew, and friends (near and far).

PREFACE

These poems come from my heart, and soul.
They came to fruition while searching for peace
in a period of constant change.

Something Magical

If you think about it,
take a moment and really think about it.
you can acknowledge the
beauty all around you.
watch as kindness
becomes the norm
again.
and feel you are part of
something magical.

We Are All The Same

We are all looking for something.
aren't we? that mystical piece
we think we are missing.
the part of us that brings peace. happiness.
calm in any type of chaos.
we may go about finding it
differently. but.
we are all the same. and ultimately.
we will find everything we are looking for.

Grateful For Today

I'm grateful today.
simply for the light. (and warmth).
the air seems fresh and crisp.
the scent of flowers. fills me up.
both with delight. (and probably pollen).
and I feel my overthinking slow down.
the weight on my shoulders is lessening.
these days are a lot sometimes.
and I'm choosing to be. grateful for today.

Allow Yourself This Moment

Listen to the silence.
let it permeate through you.
feel the soft rhythm of your heart.
beat. beat. beating.
as you breathe-slowly-
in and out.
allow yourself this moment.
of quiet. to just be.

A Reason to Be

Sometimes, I wonder where,
the me of before went. that woman
with dreams. but no follow through.
confidence in small amounts
and varying occasions.
and right now. all I can say is.
I'm proud of the changes. within.
acceptance of my capabilities.
and the hope to be more.
for isn't that what we all want?
a purpose much larger than ourselves.
and a reason to be.

Keep Being the Good

Keep moving forward.
in any way you can.
acknowledge your worth.
and keep being the good
in our world.
for goodness and light
is all we need.

Remember. Always.

may we remember. Always.
may we find gratitude. Within.
and cherish -every little bit-
of what we have. and all
we've been given.

Worthy

As humans. we often look for signs
-for how a day will be-
(or what our purpose is for).
it's often something simple-yet meaningful-
Today. a yellow butterfly. stopping before me.
perhaps at ease.
perhaps leaving a message. to remind me.
this life I live. this person I am.
is worthy. of all I desire.
and Tomorrow. I hope your sign
-finds you-
Worthy.

Moments in Silence

There are moments. in silence.
when the light comes alive. warming you.
from the -inside-
out.
and you know. without hesitation.
that life. in all its chaos.
can only get better.

Hope

Let's start each day
with hope.
which can mean different things.
Hope
for a good day.
Hope
for peace within the chaos.
Hope
for whatever you might be needing.
It's hope
that we long for. and perhaps-All-
we require.

With All My Heart

one of my favorite things
to do is love. with all my heart.
it honestly takes so little
to care about others.
it's also. one of my biggest flaws.
because I care too much. about
too many things. and sometimes. I wonder. if
that love will ever
be returned in the same way.

needless to say. I love with all my heart. and I
always will.

May Love Be

May love be
the answer
to all our prayers.
May love be
everything that brightens
our days and fills
our souls with peace.
May love be
found in the acceptance
of others. allowing them
to be. who they are.
May love be
really and truly
All we need.

A Mighty Force

she was at a loss for the words
that conveyed her strength.
and that was okay. because she knows
who she is inside and always will be.
a mighty force of a woman.

Simple Things

It's the simple things-
sunshine and coffee,
a moment of peace,
and a beautiful flower
to make a happy heart-

Sometimes, all it takes is two eyes
and a willing soul
to bring happiness to life.

Made of Light

If you're searching
for a little bit of light,
I suggest-
looking within. for,
You. are made of
more
Light
than you yet know.

Throughout Our Days

May we find delight
in the orange and black wings
of a monarch butterfly-
as it crosses our path-
May we carry that delight
throughout our days.

We Are the Sunshine

We are the sunshine
in this chaos
-called life-
long may we shine.

Be At Peace

Let's fill our days
with love
for everything around us.
Let's watch (with delight)
the blooming of a rose,
as it scent captivates us.
Let's be present
in all ways
with everyone near and far.
Let's allow ourselves grace
in the hard days
and joy in the good ones.
Let's find a bit of ourselves
in every little moment,
and be at peace.

Light In The Darkness

my mind and heart
are constantly full
of words, and hope
for the world around me.
All I want is-to be-
a light in the darkness.

Within Your Soul

may you find meaning
in the mundane,
hope in the darkness,
and love deep within
your soul.

The Melody for a Good Life

I want to be
an instrument
for good.
providing you
with the melody
for happiness
and
peace.
the calm, you search for
and desperately need.
I want to be
the melody for
a good life.